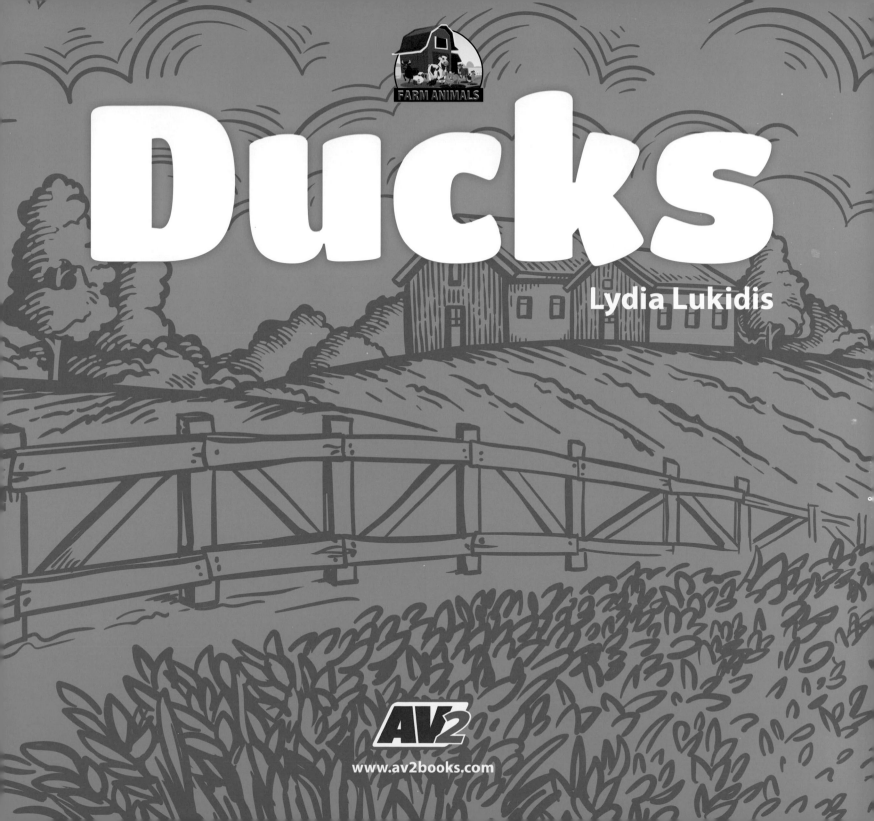

Ducks

FARM ANIMALS

Lydia Lukidis

AV2

www.av2books.com

Step 1
Go to **www.av2books.com**

Step 2
Enter this unique code

VNTLP0QMB

Step 3
Explore your interactive eBook!

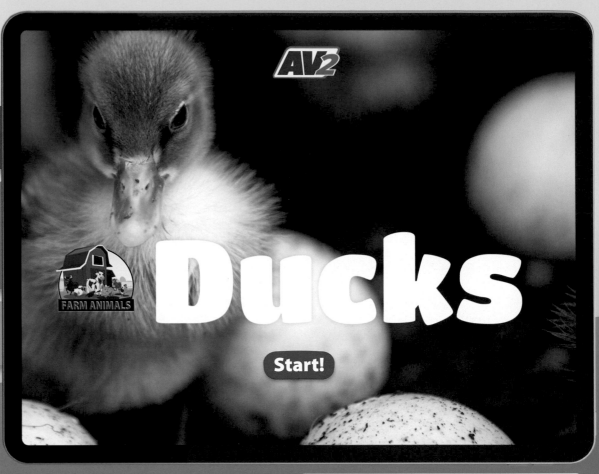

FARM ANIMALS

Ducks

Start!

Your interactive eBook comes with...

Read

Audio
Listen to the entire book read aloud

Videos
Watch informative video clips

Weblinks
Gain additional information for research

Try This!
Complete activities and hands-on experiments

Key Words
Study vocabulary, and complete a matching word activity

Quizzes
Test your knowledge

Slideshows
View images and captions

View new titles and product videos at
www.av2books.com

Ducks

Contents

Duc

A duck is a bird that lives on a farm.

Farmers keep ducks for their eggs and meat.

KS

Indiana has **more ducks** than any other state.

5

Mother ducks lay eggs.

A baby duck is called a duckling.

It takes about **30 days** for duck eggs to **hatch**.

Female ducks are called hens.

Male ducks are called drakes.

Ducks have webbed feet.

Webbed feet help them swim.

Feathers help keep ducks warm.

They also help
keep ducks dry.

Ducks talk to each other by quacking and whistling.

Ducklings follow the **sound** of their mother.

Ducks eat insects and plants.

They like berries as a treat.

Ducks will **eat** 4 to 6 ounces of food a day.

More than 20 kinds of ducks can be found on farms.

All ducks have feathers, but not all of them can fly.

Ducks enjoy living outside.

Fresh air and clean water help ducks stay healthy.

DUCK FACTS

These pages provide detailed information that expands on the interesting facts found in the book. They are intended to be used by adults as a learning support to help young readers round out their knowledge of each unique animal featured in the *Farm Animals* series and why it is kept and raised on farms.

Pages 4–5

A duck is a bird that lives on a farm. People have raised ducks for about 4,000 years. People began doing this in Southeast Asia. Scientists believe the earliest relatives of modern ducks existed millions of years ago. These prehistoric ducks roamed the planet with the dinosaurs.

Pages 6–7

Mother ducks lay eggs. Female ducks will lay one egg per day. Farm ducks can lay between 200 and 300 eggs a year. Ducklings are some of the most independent baby animals. They hatch with their eyes open and are able to walk and find their own food after a few hours.

Pages 8–9

Male ducks are called drakes. Male and female ducks have different kinds of feathers. Females usually have brown feathers. This helps them blend in with their surroundings and hide from dangerous animals. Males have brighter, more colorful feathers. This helps them attract a female partner.

Pages 10–11

Ducks have webbed feet. Duck toes are connected by a thin piece of skin. Ducks use their webbed feet like paddles to push through the water. They swim faster that way.

Pages 12–13

Feathers help keep ducks warm. Ducks have a special oil in their bodies. They cover their feathers with this oil. It prevents the ducks from getting wet. The feathers become worn out with time. Twice a year, ducks lose their feathers and grow new ones. This is called molting.

Pages 14–15

Ducks talk to each other mostly by quacking and whistling. The female mallard has the most famous quack of any duck. She can quack loudly. She calls out to other ducks that way, including her babies. Female ducks tend to make more noise than males.

Pages 16–17

Ducks eat insects and plants. In nature, ducks also eat sand and small pieces of stone. On a farm, farmers will add cracked egg or oyster shells to their food. The sharp pieces help break down their food.

Pages 18–19

More than 20 kinds of ducks can be found on a farm. Ducks belong to a group of animals called *Anatidae*. Ducks are related to swans and geese. Most ducks on farms do not fly. Farmers feed them more food than what a wild duck can find on its own. That way, farm ducks have no need to fly anywhere.

Pages 20–21

Ducks enjoy living outside. Having a pond or a lake on a farm is ideal for ducks. They drink the water and clean their feathers with it. Straw can be used for duck beds and nests. Ducks on farms can live for about 10 years.

KEY WORDS

Research has shown that as much as 65 percent of all written material published in English is made up of 300 words. These 300 words cannot be taught using pictures or learned by sounding them out. They must be recognized by sight. This book contains 50 common sight words to help young readers improve their reading fluency and comprehension. This book also teaches young readers several important content words, such as proper nouns. These words are paired with pictures to aid in learning and improve understanding.

Page	Sight Words First Appearance
4	a, and, farm, for, is, keep, lives, on, that, their
5	any, has, more, other, state, than
7	about, days, it, mother, takes, the, to
8	are
10	feet, have, help, them
13	also, they
14	by, each, talk
15	follow, of, sound
16	as, eat, like, plants, will
18	be, can, found, kinds
19	all, but, not
20	air, water

Page	Content Words First Appearance
4	bird, duck, eggs, farmers, meat
5	Indiana
7	duckling
8	hens
9	drakes
12	feathers
14	quacking, whistling
15	mother
16	berries, bugs, feed, treat
20	outside

Published by AV2
350 5th Avenue, 59th Floor New York, NY 10118
Website: www.av2books.com

Library of Congress Cataloging-in-Publication Data

Names: Lukidis, Lydia, author.
Title: Ducks / Lydia Lukidis.
Description: New York : AV2, [2019] | Series: Farm animals | Audience: Grades 2-3 |
Identifiers: LCCN 2019047983 (print) | LCCN 2019047984 (ebook) | ISBN 9781791116484 (library binding) | ISBN 9781791116491 (paperback) | ISBN 9781791116507 (ebook other) | ISBN 9781791116514 (ebook other)
Subjects: LCSH: Ducks--Juvenile literature.
Classification: LCC SF505.3 .L85 2019 (print) | LCC SF505.3 (ebook) | DDC 636.5/97--dc23
LC record available at https://lccn.loc.gov/2019047983
LC ebook record available at https://lccn.loc.gov/2019047984

Printed in Guangzhou, China
1 2 3 4 5 6 7 8 9 0 24 23 22 21 20

022020
100919

Art Director: Terry Paulhus   Project Coordinators: Sara Cucini and Ryan Smith

Every reasonable effort has been made to trace ownership and to obtain permission to reprint copyright material. The publisher would be pleased to have any errors or omissions brought to its attention so that they may be corrected in subsequent printings.

AV2 acknowledges Shutterstock, iStock, and Alamy as the primary image suppliers for this title.